Packing a healthy breakfast for kids can be challenging, especially when busy schedules make it difficult to find time to prepare meals. However, there are many quick and easy recipes that can provide your child with the energy they need to start their day right. Here are some of our favorite healthy breakfast ideas for kids

OVERNIGHT OATS

Overnight oats are a great way to make sure your child's breakfast is ready when they wake up – just combine rolled oats, milk, and yogurt in a mason jar the night before and let it sit overnight. In the morning, you can add fresh fruit for extra flavor.

Fruit smoothies

Let's make a smoothie for your kids. Fruit smoothies are easy to make and perfect for breakfast or snack time. Here's what you will need:
-Frozen fruit such as strawberries, blueberries, bananas or peaches (or any other desired fruits)
-Yogurt
-Milk
-Sugar/honey/maple syrup (optional)
Start by adding frozen fruit into a blender. Add yogurt and milk to cover the fruit - about 1 cup of yogurt and 1 cup of milk per serving is good. If needed, add sugar/honey

Strawberry Toast

Strawberry Toast is a healthy and tasty breakfast option for kids that's easy to prepare. To make it, start by melting the butter in a medium-sized skillet over medium heat. Add the sliced strawberries and cook for 5 minutes or until the berries have softened. Next, add the maple syrup, orange zest, non-fat milk, and teaspoon of salt. Cook for another 3 minutes or until the mixture thickens. Finally, place the slices of cinnamon raisin bread in a single layer on top of the strawberry mixture. Crack three eggs over the toast and let cook until the whites are set and yolks have just started to become soft. Serve immediately with a sprinkle of extra orange zest. Enjoy!

Egg Muffins

When it comes to baking, there are many options to choose from that will tantalize your taste buds. From cakes and cupcakes, to muffins and brownies, there's something for everyone. But one of the most popular treats is the classic egg muffin. Egg muffins are quick and easy to make and perfect for breakfast on-the-go. Here's what you'll need:

- -Eggs
- -Milk
- -Cheese
- -Veggies of your choice (onion, bell peppers, mushrooms, spinach are all great options)
- -Butter or oil for cooking
- -Salt and pepper to taste.

Start by preheating the oven to 375 degrees F and greasing a muffin pan with butter or oil. In a large bowl, whisk together eggs, milk, cheese and veggies. Fill each muffin cup about 3/4 full with egg mixture and season with salt and pepper to taste. Bake for 25 minutes or until egg is set. Enjoy! With egg muffins you can have a delicious breakfast ready in no time

Scrambled Eggs

Eggs are one of the best sources of protein to start the day and scrambled eggs take just minutes to make. Just whisk eggs with milk, season with salt and pepper, and fry them in a non-stick pan for an easy breakfast that your child will love.

Oatmeal Pancakes

Ingredients:
- 1 cup old-fashioned rolled oats
- 1 cup milk, regular or non-dairy
- 2 large eggs
- 1 tablespoon unsalted butter, plus more for cooking
- 1 tablespoon granulated sugar
- 2/3 cup all-purpose flour
- 2 teaspoons baking powder
- 1/4 teaspoon kosher salt
- 1/4 teaspoon ground cinnamon (optional)

- **Instructions:**
- 1. In a medium bowl, combine the oats and milk and let stand for 10 minutes.
- 2. In a small bowl, whisk together the eggs, butter, and sugar until light and fluffy.
- 3. Add the egg mixture to the oats mixture and stir until combined.
- 4. In a separate bowl, sift together the flour, baking powder, salt, and cinnamon (if using).
- 5. Add the dry ingredients to the wet ingredients in two batches and mix until just combined – do not overmix!
- 6. Heat a non-stick frying pan over

Breakfast Grilled Cheese

Grilled cheese sandwiches are a classic favorite, made of two slices of bread with melted cheese in the middle. But what if you want to take your grilled cheese up a notch? Try adding egg and sausage! Start by cooking some diced sausage in a pan until it's fully cooked through. Then, crack an egg into the same pan and scramble it with the sausage until both ingredients are thoroughly mixed together. Spread this egg-sausage mix onto half of one slice of bread and then cover it with plenty of grated cheese before adding another piece of bread on top. Place the sandwich in a heated skillet over medium heat for about 3 minutes each side or until the bread is golden brown and the cheese has melted completely. Enjoy this egg and sausage-filled grilled cheese sandwich with your favorite condiments

A grilled cheese sandwich is a simple and tasty meal. With egg and sausage added, it can be an even more delicious treat that the whole family will love. Don't forget to enjoy your egg and sausage grilled cheese sandwich!

Guacamole Toast
Ingredients:

- ripe avocados.
- Juice of 1 lime.
- 1/2 tsp. kosher salt.
- 1/2 c. cherry tomatoes, quartered.
- 1/2. small red onion, minced.
- 1/2. jalapeño, minced.
- clove garlic, minced.
- slices sourdough bread, toasted.

To make the guacamole, start by mashing the ripe avocados in a bowl. Add the juice of one lime and 1/2 teaspoon of kosher salt. Gently mix in the cherry tomatoes, red onion, jalapeño, and garlic. Serve your freshly made guacamole with slices of toasted sourdough bread for a delicious snack! Enjoy!

For an extra flavor boost, try adding diced mango or cilantro! The possibilities are endless! Whatever combination you choose will be sure to add some pizzazz to your homemade guacamole. Experiment away and share your creations with friends and family!

Happy snacking!

Homemade Granola

This healthy breakfast is perfect for kids and adults alike. It's quick and easy to make, requiring only four simple ingredients: almond butter, chopped walnuts, unsweetened coconut flakes, and dried cranberries. The combination of healthy fats from the almond butter and nuts, fiber from the coconut flakes, and natural sweetness from the cranberries makes it a great start to your day. Enjoy it as a healthy snack throughout the day too! This healthy breakfast is sure to please everyone in the family.

To make it, start by combining the almond butter and chopped walnuts in a medium bowl. Stir until they are well combined. Then add in the coconut flakes and dried cranberries, stirring until everything is evenly distributed. Serve with your favorite healthy breakfast items like fresh fruits or yogurt for a nutritious start to the day. Enjoy!

Peanut Butter Pancakes

Ingredients

250g crunchy peanut butter.
50g unsalted butter, cubed, plus extra for cooking.
6 tbsp maple syrup.
300g self-raising flour.
1 tsp baking powder.
1 tbsp golden caster sugar.
2 large eggs.
350ml milk.

1. In a medium saucepan, melt the peanut butter and butter over low-medium heat until completely combined.
2. Add in the maple syrup, stirring frequently until fully incorporated. Set aside to cool slightly.
3. Combine the flour, baking powder and sugar in a large bowl and stir to combine.
4. In a separate bowl whisk together the eggs and milk until light and frothy, then add this to the dry ingredients along with the cooled peanut butter mixture. Stir together until just combined; don't over mix as this will make your pancakes tough!
5. Heat a non-stick frying pan over medium heat and lightly grease

Waffles

Ingredients

1 ¾ cups unbleached all purpose flour.
1 tablespoon baking powder.
1 tablespoon sugar.
½ teaspoon salt.
3 eggs.
8 tablespoon butter melted and cooled to
room temp. I like to use the olive oil and butter
blend sticks.
1 ½ cups 2% milk.

Waffles are a great and healthy breakfast for kids! Start by gathering all the ingredients you need: 1 ¾ cups unbleached all purpose flour, 1 tablespoon baking powder, 1 tablespoon sugar, ½ teaspoon salt, 3 eggs, 8 tablespoons butter melted and cooled to room temperature (you can use an olive oil and butter blend sticks), and 1 ½ cups 2% milk. In a medium bowl mix together the flour, baking powder, sugar and salt. In a separate bowl whisk together the eggs and then add in the melted butter and milk. Pour this egg mixture over the dry ingredients while whisking until completely blended. Now your waffle batter is ready to be cooked! Heat up your waffle maker according to its instructions and pour some of the batter in. After a few minutes you'll have delicious and healthy waffles for your kids to enjoy! Enjoy!

Enjoying waffles is a great way to start the day off on the right foot with a healthy breakfast for your kids. With just a few ingredients, you can whip up a batch of delicious waffles that will be sure to please even the pickiest of eaters. By following our simple instructions you'll be able to create tasty and nutritious waffles in no time! So what are you waiting for? Get cooking and enjoy this yummy breakfast treat!

Cocoa Cake

Ingredients

2 cups (240g) all-purpose flour.
3/4 cup (64g) unsweetened cocoa powder.
1 & 1/4 teaspoons baking soda.
3/4 teaspoon salt.
3/4 cup (170g) unsalted butter, softened.
1 & 3/4 cups (350g) firmly packed light
brown sugar.
2 large eggs.
1 & 1/3 cups (314ml) water.!

To make the cocoa cake, start by preheating the oven to 350°F (177°C). Grease and flour a 9 x 13-inch baking pan. In a medium bowl, whisk together the all-purpose flour, cocoa powder, baking soda and salt until evenly combined. In a large bowl using an electric mixer on medium speed, cream together the butter and brown sugar until light and fluffy. Add in the eggs one at a time, beating well after each addition. Gradually add in the dry ingredients in three batches alternately with water in two batches until just combined. Pour into prepared pan and bake for about 40 minutes or until toothpick inserted into center comes out clean. Allow cake to cool completely before serving. Enjoy

Quesadillas

Ingredients
- 1 whole-grain flour tortilla (about 8" diameter)
- ½ cup freshly grated cheddar cheese.
- ¼ cup cooked black beans or pinto beans, rinsed and drained.
- 1 tablespoon chopped red bell pepper or jarred roasted bell pepper or a few thinly sliced cherry tomatoes.
- 1 tablespoon chopped red onion or green onion.

Quesadillas are a healthy and delicious breakfast option for kids. With only four ingredients, it is easy to prepare with minimal effort. To make quesadillas, begin by taking one whole-grain flour tortilla (about 8" diameter) and spreading ½ cup freshly grated cheddar cheese over one side of the tortilla. Then add ¼ cup cooked black beans or pinto beans, rinsed and drained, 1 tablespoon chopped red bell pepper or jarred roasted bell pepper, and 1 tablespoon chopped red onion or green onion on top of the cheese. Lastly, fold the un-cheese side of the tortilla onto the cheese side. Heat a skillet over medium heat and cook until both sides are golden brown and the cheese is melted. Cut into wedges and enjoy! Quesadillas are a healthy, protein-packed breakfast that kids will love!

Alternatively, you can also prepare quesadilla fillings ahead of time and store in the fridge for quickly assembling in the morning. Fill your tortilla with ¼ cup cooked black beans or pinto beans, rinsed and drained, 1 tablespoon chopped red bell pepper or jarred roasted bell pepper, 1 tablespoon chopped red onion or green onion and ½ cup freshly grated cheddar cheese. Wrap each filled tortilla in plastic wrap and place in an airtight container. In the morning, just heat up one quesadilla per person at a time until golden brown and serve

Green Smoothie

Ingredients

Milk- 1 1/2 cup of milk, or any nut
milk.
Spinach- 2 cups fully packed.
Banana- 1 banana (frozen is best)
Apple- 1 apple sliced into pieces.
Avocado- 1/4 avocado.

Green smoothies are a healthy and delicious breakfast option for kids. Preparing this nutrient-packed treat is easy – add all of the ingredients to a blender, blend until creamy, and serve!

To make your green smoothie, start by gathering 1 1/2 cups of milk (or any nut milk), 2 cups fully packed spinach, 1 banana (frozen is best), 1 apple sliced into pieces, and 1/4 avocado. Place these ingredients into a blender, and blend until the mixture reaches a creamy consistency. It's now ready to serve!

This healthy breakfast choice is filled with essential vitamins such as vitamin A from spinach and healthy fats from avocado. Not only will it provide lasting energy for your

Classic Eggs Benedict

Ingredients

1 1/2 tablespoons white vinegar
8 large eggs
8 ounces thinly sliced smoked ham
4 English muffins (split and toasted)
2 tablespoons chopped fresh chives

Egg Benedict is a classic dish that is sure to please the whole family. The combination of healthy ingredients, such as smoked ham, eggs and English muffins, create a delicious and nutritious breakfast. Kids will love the flavor of this simple meal and it provides them with important sources of protein and vitamins. Plus, you can easily customize Egg Benedict by adding fresh herbs such as chives or substituting the smoked ham for bacon or turkey. Just don't forget the white vinegar which helps give this dish its signature flavor! With just a few ingredients, you can quickly whip up an amazing egg benedict breakfast that your kids will love!

Instructions:

1. In a medium bowl, whisk together 1 1/2 tablespoons white vinegar and 8 large eggs.

2. Heat a wide, non-stick pan over medium heat and add the egg mixture when it is hot. Cook for 2 minutes until the bottom layer has set before stirring gently with a spatula to scramble the eggs. Cook until all of the eggs are cooked through and set aside in a warm place.

3. Toast 4 English muffins in a toaster or under the broiler until golden brown and cut each into halves. Place each half onto individual plates.

4. Place 8 ounces thinly sliced smoked ham on top of the toasted English muffins.

5. Divide the cooked eggs among the four plates and sprinkle with 2 tablespoons chopped fresh chives.

6. Serve warm and enjoy!

Fruit Salad

Ingredients

4 cups fresh pineapple chunks.
1 qt. strawberries, hulled and sliced in half.
3 cups seedless green grapes.
2 mangoes, peeled and sliced.
2 (4-oz.) containers fresh raspberries.
2 cups Greek yogurt.
1 tablespoon dark brown sugar.
1 tablespoon honey.

Fruit salad is a great option for a healthy breakfast for kids. With the right ingredients, you can make a delicious and nutritious meal that everyone in your family will enjoy.

To make this fruit salad, start by combining the pineapple chunks, strawberries, green grapes, mangoes and raspberries in a large bowl. Stir to combine all of the fruits evenly. In a separate small bowl, mix together the Greek yogurt with dark brown sugar and honey until fully combined. Gently fold this mixture into the fruit until it is evenly distributed throughout. Refrigerate the salad for at least 30 minutes before serving so that all of the flavors have time to mingle together. Serve chilled or at room temperature as desired. Enjoy!

Chia Budding

Ingredients

1 14 ounce can unsweetened light coconut milk.
1 cup plain fat-free Greek yogurt.
2 tablespoon pure maple syrup.
½ teaspoon vanilla.
¼ cup chia seeds.
2 cup chopped fresh fruit or berries, such as pineapple, strawberries,
blueberries, raspberries, mango, and/or peach)

Chia budding is a healthy and easy breakfast that can be prepared quickly. It's perfect for busy parents who want to give their kids a healthy start to the day.

To prepare chia budding, you'll need 1 14 ounce can of unsweetened light coconut milk, 1 cup of plain fat-free Greek yogurt, 2 tablespoons of pure maple syrup, ½ teaspoon of vanilla extract and ¼ cup of chia seeds. Combine the ingredients in a bowl until everything is thoroughly mixed together. Then add the chopped fresh fruit or berries - such as pineapple, strawberries, blueberries, raspberries, mango and/or peach - and stir again until everything is evenly distributed.

Spoon the mixture into individual serving dishes, cover, and refrigerate overnight. In the morning, your chia pudding will be ready to enjoy! It's a healthy and delicious breakfast that both kids and adults can enjoy. Enjoy!

French Toast

ingredients 4 Servings

1 egg.
1 teaspoon McCormick® All
Natural Pure Vanilla Extract.
1/2 teaspoon McCormick®
Ground Cinnamon.
1/4 cup milk.
4 slices bread.

This recipe for French Toast is an easy and healthy breakfast option for kids. It's full of great flavors from the McCormick® All Natural Pure Vanilla Extract, McCormick® Ground Cinnamon, egg, and milk. The instructions are as follows:

1. In a shallow bowl, beat together the egg, vanilla extract, cinnamon and milk until they are well combined.
2. Dip each slice of bread into the egg mixture and turn the slice to coat both sides evenly with the mixture.
3. Heat a lightly oiled griddle or frying pan over medium heat. Place the coated slices of bread on the pan and cook on each side until golden brown (about two minutes). Serve warm with desired toppings such as syrup, jam or honey.

Enjoy this delicious French Toast as a healthy breakfast for kids! It's sure to be a hit with everyone in the family. Bon appétit!

Fried Eggs And Bacon

Ingredients

4large eggs.
8bacon slices.
Kosher salt and freshly
ground black pepper.
Toast, for serving.

Are you looking for an easy, healthy breakfast for your kids? Look no further than this delicious bacon and fried egg dish! It's packed with healthy protein and fats to give them the boost they need in the morning. Plus, it takes just minutes to prepare.

To make this healthy breakfast, start by frying 8 bacon slices over medium-high heat until crisp. Transfer the cooked bacon slices to a plate lined with paper towels to absorb any excess fat. Then, crack 4 large eggs into the hot pan and season with kosher salt and freshly ground black pepper. Fry on both sides until lightly browned and done to your liking. Serve immediately with toast for an easy yet healthy breakfast that will keep them full throughout the morning. Enjoy!

Scrambled Eggs Wrap!

Ingredients

1 or 2 large eggs.
1 or 2 tbsp milk (2%) or water.
Salt.
Pepper.
1-2 tbsp canola oil.
1 flour tortilla (8 inch)
2 tbsp shredded Cheddar cheese.
1 tbsp salsa.

Scrambled eggs wraps make a healthy and easy breakfast for kids. To prepare the wrap, start by cracking the eggs into a bowl. Add the milk (or water) and season with salt and pepper to taste. Heat oil in a non-stick pan over medium heat. Pour in the egg mixture and stir until scrambled, then remove from heat. Place tortilla on a flat surface and sprinkle with cheese, then spoon salsa onto one half of it. Add scrambled eggs to the other side of tortilla, fold it over and press lightly to seal. Enjoy! This tasty wrap can be served hot or cold, so it's perfect for busy mornings when you need something nutritious quickly!

Banana Baked Oatmeal

Ingredients
2 cups rolled oats.
½ cup pecan pieces (optional)
1 teaspoon baking powder.
1 ½ teaspoons cinnamon.
½ teaspoon allspice.
½ teaspoon kosher salt.
¾ cup mashed banana or 2 very ripe bananas.
1 ¾ cups milk of choice (dairy, almond or oat)

If you're looking for something warm and healthy to make your kids in the morning, try banana baked oatmeal! Start by preheating the oven to 350F (180C). In a bowl, mix together the rolled oats, pecan pieces (optional), baking powder, cinnamon, allspice and salt. Add in mashed banana or two very ripe bananas and milk of choice (dairy, almond or oat) and stir until everything is combined. Spread this mixture into an 8x8 inch baking dish and bake for 35 minutes. Let cool before serving. This delicious breakfast option can be served with yogurt or fruit for an extra healthy boost! Kids will love it!

Quiche with Spinach And Cheese

Ingredients

1/2 recipe homemade pie crust*
1 (10 oz) box frozen spinach*
8 oz fresh mushrooms, sliced.
1 teaspoon minced garlic (or roasted & chopped)
4 large eggs.
1 cup whole milk*
1/3 cup grated parmesan cheese.
1 cup shredded cheese (I used cheddar +
mozzarella)*

Quiche with spinach and cheese is a healthy breakfast option that's simple to prepare. With only a few ingredients, you can have this tasty dish ready in no time! The combination of greens and cheese make it an ideal dish for kids. To get started, preheat your oven to 375°F (190°C).

Begin by preparing the pie crust according to recipe instructions or using store-bought pastry. Once the crust is ready, spread the frozen spinach evenly over the bottom of the tart shell. Then top with mushrooms and garlic.

In a medium bowl, whisk together eggs, milk and parmesan cheese until combined. Pour egg mixture over vegetables in crust then sprinkle shredded cheese on top. Place quiche on a baking sheet and bake for 25 minutes or until the center is set and cheese is golden brown.

Allow quiche to cool slightly before serving. Enjoy!

Quiche Lorraine

ingredients

Pastry for a one-crust nine-inch pie (see pastry recipe)
4strips bacon.
1onion, thinly sliced.
1cup Gruyère or Swiss cheese, cubed.
¼cup grated Parmesan cheese.
4eggs, lightly beaten.
2cups heavy cream or 1 cup each milk and cream.
¼teaspoon nutmeg.!

Quiche Lorraine is a healthy breakfast for kids that can be made easily with ingredients that you likely already have in your kitchen. To make the quiche, begin by preheating your oven to 375°F and preparing a pastry crust following the recipe linked above. Once your pastry has been rolled out, cut four strips of bacon into small cubes and cook them in a pan over medium heat until they are browned and crisp. Then, add thinly sliced onions to the same pan and cook until they are softened. In a bowl, combine the Gruyère or Swiss cheese cubes and Parmesan cheese with the cooked bacon and onions. Pour this mixture into the prepared crust.

In another bowl, whisk together eggs, cream (or a combination of milk and cream), and nutmeg. Pour the egg mixture over the cheese, bacon, and onion in the crust. Bake at 375°F for 35 minutes or until golden brown and a knife inserted into the center comes out clean. Enjoy your quiche lorraine as a healthy breakfast for kids!

English Breakfast

A healthy breakfast for kids doesn't have to be complicated or time consuming. A classic English breakfast can be a great option, providing all of the necessary nutrients for growing children in an enjoyable way. All you need is bacon, eggs, sausage, black pudding (optional), baked beans, grilled tomatoes and fried bread or toast. Serve it with healthy accompaniments such as jams, marmalades and fresh orange juice. When preparing an English breakfast for kids ensure that the ingredients are cooked properly and that any meat products are well done before serving. Breakfast is a key meal of the day so take your time to make sure you provide healthy options for your family. The traditional English breakfast can be a nutritious start to their day!

Apple Muffins

With just a few simple ingredients, you can make healthy apple muffins that are perfect for a quick breakfast or snack. Whether you're feeding kids or just looking for an easy-to-make healthy treat, these muffins are sure to be a hit!

To prepare the apple muffins, begin by preheating your oven to 350 degrees Fahrenheit. In a large bowl, combine 2 cups of sugar, 2 eggs, and 1 cup of oil like vegetable, canola, or coconut oil. Then add in 1 tablespoon of vanilla extract. In a separate bowl mix together 3 cups all-purpose flour with 1 teaspoon each of salt, baking soda, and cinnamon. Gradually stir the dry ingredients into the wet ones until both are fully combined.

Fold in 2 cups of diced apples, then spoon the muffin batter into greased or paper-lined muffin tins. Bake the muffins on the center rack in your preheated 350 degree oven for 20 to 25 minutes or until a wooden toothpick inserted into the center comes out clean. Let the muffins cool on a wire cooling rack before serving and enjoy!

The healthy apple muffins are great as a quick breakfast option for kids or as an afternoon snack. They're also delicious served warm with a pat of butter or cream cheese. Make sure to store any leftover muffins in an airtight container at room temperature for up to 4 days. Enjoy!

Banana Bread

Banana bread is a healthy and delicious breakfast option for kids. It is filled with energy-boosting healthy ingredients like ripe bananas, flour, sugar, salt, baking soda, vanilla extract and softened butter. If you want to make it an even heartier and more flavorful meal, you can also add walnuts and raisins to turn it into banana nut bread.

Making banana bread is easy! Start by preheating your oven to 350 degrees Fahrenheit. In one bowl mix together the dry ingredients - flour, sugar, salt and baking soda - until they are well combined. In another bowl mash the ripe bananas until smooth then stir in softened butter, eggs and vanilla extract until everything is fully incorporated. Combine the wet ingredients with the dry ingredients and fold together. Lastly, if desired, mix in walnuts and raisins.

Once everything is blended, pour the batter into a greased loaf pan and bake for 50-60 minutes or until a toothpick inserted into the middle comes out clean. Serve warm with butter or cream cheese - enjoy!

Banana bread makes a healthy breakfast for kids that is sure to please everyone in the family. Try making it today for an easy and healthy start to any day!

Tofu Scramble

Ingredients

1 tablespoon olive oil.
(1) 16-ounce block firm tofu.
2 tablespoons nutritional yeast.
1/2 teaspoon salt, or more to taste.
1/4 teaspoon turmeric.
1/4 teaspoon garlic powder.
2 tablespoons non-dairy milk,
unsweetened and unflavored.

ofu scramble is a healthy breakfast for kids that can be easily prepared with just a few ingredients. To make the tofu scramble, first heat the olive oil in a non-stick skillet over medium-high heat. Next, crumble the block of firm tofu into small pieces and add it to the pan. Stir in the nutritional yeast, salt, turmeric, garlic powder and non-dairy milk. Cook for about 8 minutes or until desired texture is reached. Serve with cooked vegetables such as bell peppers, onions and mushrooms for extra flavor and nutrition. Enjoy!

Tofu scramble is an easy way to start your day off healthy while providing your children with all the essential nutrients they need to keep their energy levels up

Cottage Cheese Breakfast Bowl

Cottage cheese breakfast bowls are healthy and easy to prepare, making them a great breakfast option for kids. To make this healthy morning meal, add ¾ cup of cottage cheese to a bowl. All brands will taste different, so experiment until you find the one that you like best. After adding the cottage cheese, top it with fresh berries or diced apple for flavor and texture. In this example bowl, blueberries, raspberries and blackberries were used. For an extra crunchy topping, add a sprinkle of chopped nuts such as almonds or walnuts. For added sweetness, stir in a pinch of cinnamon and drizzle honey over top before serving. Enjoy!
When prepared correctly, cottage cheese breakfast bowls are healthy options for your family's breakfast routine.
For a healthy, tasty and easy-to-prepare breakfast, try cottage cheese bowls!
Start your day with this healthy meal that the whole family can enjoy.

Cottage cheese breakfast bowls are a nutritious way to start off the day. Not only are they healthy, but they're also incredibly simple to make. Simply add ¾ cup of cottage cheese to a bowl and find one that you love since different brands have different tastes. Topping it off with fresh berries such as blueberries, raspberries and blackberries adds flavor and texture to the dish. Go for an extra crunchy topping by adding chopped nuts like almonds or walnuts on top. Adding a pinch of cinnamon and a drizzle of honey will give it an extra sweet touch. With this healthy breakfast, your kids are sure to start their day off right!
So don't be afraid to whip up a healthy cottage cheese breakfast bowl for your family's morning routine! Enjoy the delicious flavors that come with it and feel good knowing that you're giving your kids an energizing start to the day.
Enjoy this healthy meal and fuel up with a nutritious breakfast every day. Bon Appetit!

Smoked Salmon Toast

Ingredients
1 ripe avocado.
1 tablespoon crème fraîche.
1 lemon.
70 g radishes.
3 sprigs of fresh dill.
1 tablespoon cider vinegar.
12-16 slices of crispbread or thinly sliced and toasted rye bread.
200 g smoked salmon , from sustainable sources.

Smoked Salmon Toast is a healthy and delicious breakfast option for kids. It's easy to prepare, with just a few simple ingredients - ripe avocado, crème fraîche, lemon, radishes, fresh dill, cider vinegar, crispbread or thinly sliced and toasted rye bread and smoked salmon.

To make the toast: Start by slicing the avocado into thin slices and arranging them on top of the toast. Mix together the crème fraîche with some freshly squeezed lemon juice until combined. Spread this mixture over the avocado slices. Slice the radishes into thin rounds and arrange them around each slice of toast. Sprinkle some finely chopped dill onto each slice of toast. Drizzle over some cider vinegar and top with some smoked salmon.

Serve the Smoked Salmon Toast for a healthy and delicious breakfast for kids. Enjoy!

Cottage Cheese Pancakes

To begin making your cottage cheese pancakes, whisk together the cottage cheese and eggs until all the lumps are gone. Then add in the vanilla extract, sugar, baking powder and flour. Whisk until everything is well incorporated. Finally add in the canola oil and mix until combined.

Heat a skillet to medium heat and pour 1/4 cup of the batter onto the pan. Cook until small bubbles start to form around the edge, then carefully flip over with a spatula and cook for another 2-3 minutes. Serve your cottage cheese pancakes hot with butter or syrup. Enjoy!

These healthy pancakes are sure to provide your kids with the energy they need for their busy days ahead. You can even add in some fruit, nuts or chocolate chips for an extra special treat! With just a few simple steps you can have a healthy breakfast ready in no time. Give them a try today!

Almond Butter Toast

Ingredients

2 pieces of Wholegrain Loaf cut into 1/2" slices.
4 Tbsp almond Butter.
1/2 Tbsp pumpkin Seeds.
1/2 cup raspberries.
8 fresh mint leaves.
1 Tsp chia seeds.

To begin making your healthy breakfast for kids, spread a generous amount of almond butter onto each piece of bread. Top with the pumpkin seeds, raspberries and mint leaves before sprinkling with chia seeds. Toast the slices of bread in a toaster for 2-3 minutes or until golden brown. Serve your healthy toast hot and enjoy!

Your kids will love eating this healthy breakfast that is packed with protein, healthy fats and antioxidants. It's sure to provide them with everything they need to start their day off right. Give it a try today!

With these healthy and delicious breakfast options, your kids are sure to have the energy they need throughout their day while also getting all the essential nutrients they need. Enjoy!

Homemade Acai Bowl

A healthy breakfast for kids doesn't have to be a chore. With the right ingredients, you can easily whip up an Acai Bowl that is packed with nutrition and flavor. An Acai Bowl is made from frozen pureed acai berries, banana, pineapple, mixed berries, Greek yogurt, almond milk and honey.

To prepare your Acai Bowl, start by slightly thawing 1 cup of frozen acai puree in the microwave or a bowl of warm water. Peel the banana and cut it into small slices before adding it to the mix along with 1/4 cup pineapple pieces. Then add 1 cup of frozen mixed berries and stir everything up until combined. Add in 1/4 cup of plain low-fat Greek yogurt and 1/4 cup of almond milk, and finish off with a tablespoon of honey for sweetness.

Once everything is blended together, it's time to serve the Acai Bowl. You can opt to top it with fresh fruit such as strawberries or blueberries for an added healthy boost. Enjoy your healthy and delicious Acai Bowl!

Classic Omelette

The classic omelette is a healthy and delicious breakfast option for kids. It's easy to prepare and can be served with some of their favorite toppings like chopped chives, sliced tomato, or buttered toast. Here's how you can make it:

- Crack the eggs into a bowl and beat them together until they are just blended.
- Heat the butter in a medium nonstick skillet over medium heat until melted and foamy.
- Pour the eggs into the pan and cook, stirring occasionally, until just set.
- Sprinkle with cheddar cheese, season with salt and pepper to taste, and cook for another minute or two until cheese is melted.

- Fold the omelette in half and serve with your favorite toppings.

This healthy breakfast option is sure to be a hit with kids. Enjoy!

Pecan Energy Bars

Pecan energy bars make an excellent healthy breakfast for kids. This quick and easy snack is prepared in a few simple steps:

1. Pit the dates and place them in a food processor, adding the pecans, oats, chia seeds, vanilla extract, cinnamon and salt. Pulse until everything is combined into a thick paste.

2. Line a baking dish with parchment paper and press the mixture into it evenly, making sure that all the edges are sealed.

3. Refrigerate for two hours or until set, then cut into bars and enjoy! Store any extra energy bars in an airtight container in the refrigerator for up to one week.

Pecan energy bars make a healthy, nutritious breakfast for kids that will jump-start their day with healthy ingredients like dates, pecans and oats. Enjoy!

Banana Oatmeal Pancakes

Ingredients

2 medium ripe bananas (best when they have lots of brown spots)
2 eggs.
1/2 cup unsweetened almond milk.
1 teaspoon vanilla extract.
1 ½ cups old fashioned rolled oats, gluten free if desired.
2 teaspoons baking powder.
½ teaspoon ground cinnamon.
¼ teaspoon salt.

- Start by mashing two ripe bananas in a bowl until they become smooth and creamy.

- Add two eggs and whisk until all ingredients are combined.

- Pour in the almond milk and vanilla extract, mixing together until everything is evenly distributed.

- In a separate bowl, mix the oats, baking powder, cinnamon, and salt together.

- Gradually add the dry ingredients to the wet ingredients while stirring continuously with a spoon.

- Heat a non-stick pan over medium heat and pour some of the batter onto the pan. Cook each side for about 2 minutes until golden brown.

- Serve hot with syrup or your favorite topping, and enjoy!

These healthy banana oatmeal pancakes are sure to be loved by kids while providing them with important nutrients that they need to start the day. Try making this healthy breakfast today and let your kids enjoy a delicious and healthy meal!

Avocado Toast With Egg

Avocado toast with egg is an easy and healthy breakfast option for kids. With only a few ingredients, it can be prepared quickly, making it the perfect meal to start off their day.

To prepare avocado toast with egg, first toast one slice of whole grain or gluten-free bread. Spread mashed avocado onto the toast, then spray a pan with cooking spray and crack one large egg into the center. Season with salt and pepper to taste, then cook over medium heat until the egg is done. Serve with hot sauce or red pepper flakes, if desired.

This healthy breakfast option is packed with healthy fats from the avocado and protein from the egg. Kids will love the flavor and the nutritious ingredients that make up this simple yet delicious breakfast option. Enjoy!

Scrambled Eggs With Cottage Cheese

Scrambled eggs with cottage cheese make a healthy and delicious breakfast for kids. Preparing the dish is simple, and all you need are 4 large eggs, 1/2 cup 2% cottage cheese (we recommend Good Culture), 1/8 teaspoon of kosher salt, some fresh ground black pepper, and olive oil spray.

To begin, crack the eggs into a bowl and beat until they are scrambled. Then, pour the cottage cheese into the mix and add in the salt and pepper. Spray some olive oil onto a non-stick pan over low heat and pour in the egg mixture. Stir frequently with a spatula to ensure that no part of the scramble is sticking to the pan. Cook until the eggs are just set, about 5 minutes. Serve hot and enjoy!

Scrambled eggs with cottage cheese is a healthy breakfast that your kids will love! It is packed with protein and also provides important vitamins and minerals like vitamin A, B-vitamins, phosphorus, selenium, and zinc. Plus, this dish comes together quickly and easily, so you can enjoy a healthy breakfast in no time.

Try making scrambled eggs with cottage cheese today and see how easy it is to provide your kids with a nutritious start to the day!

Easy Oatmeal Bars

Ingredients

1 cup creamy peanut butter (no sugar added, or sunflower butter for nut free)
½ cup honey (or agave syrup* for vegan)
4 cups Old Fashioned rolled oats.
½ teaspoon kosher salt.
½ teaspoon cinnamon.

These healthy and easy oatmeal bars make a great breakfast for kids. They are filled with healthy ingredients like peanut butter, honey or agave syrup, rolled oats, salt and cinnamon. Plus they can be made in advance and stored in the refrigerator or freezer!

To prepare the oatmeal bars, start by combining the creamy peanut butter, honey or agave syrup, rolled oats, salt and cinnamon in a large bowl. Mix until the ingredients are thoroughly combined. Line an 8x8 inch baking dish with parchment paper and spread the mixture evenly on top. Use your hands or the back of a spoon to press the mixture down into an even layer. Bake in a preheated 350F oven for 18-20 minutes. Allow to cool completely before cutting into bars. Enjoy!

Overnight Oats

Overnight oats are a healthy and delicious breakfast option for kids. They are easy to prepare, require minimal ingredients, and can be customized with your favorite fruits and flavors. To make overnight oats, you'll need rolled oats, milk of your choice (dairy or non-dairy works), a sweetener such as honey or maple syrup, and fresh fruit of your choice.

First, mix together the oats, milk and sweetener in a container with a tight-fitting lid. Stir everything together until evenly combined. Next, layer some chopped up fresh fruit of your choice on top of the oat mixture. Seal the container and put it in the fridge overnight to allow all the flavors to meld together.

In the morning, your healthy breakfast will be ready! You can eat it cold or heat it up in the microwave or stovetop. Add a dollop of yogurt and a sprinkle of nuts for some extra flavor and texture. Enjoy your healthy breakfast!

Breakfast Tacos

Breakfast tacos are a healthy and delicious breakfast option for kids, and they're easy to prepare too. To make healthy breakfast tacos, start by warming tortillas over medium heat in a skillet. Then add scrambled eggs to the center of the tortilla and top with green onion, crumbled bacon, diced avocado, cheddar cheese, and fresh cilantro. Season with salt and pepper to your liking. Serve the tacos while they're still warm and enjoy! Breakfast tacos are sure to be a hit with the whole family. Try experimenting with different ingredients and seasoning combinations for a fun breakfast experience every time.

This healthy, delicious breakfast option is sure to become a fast favorite in your household! Breakfast tacos are quick to put together, healthy and packed with flavor - what more could you want? So why not start the day off right by making healthy breakfast tacos for the whole family today!

With this simple recipe, healthy breakfast tacos can be a part of your regular morning routine. Give it a try and enjoy a healthy, delicious breakfast the whole family will love. Bon appetit!

Breafast Mini Frittatas

Mini Frittatas make a healthy, delicious breakfast for kids and adults alike. Preparing them is easy - all you need are some basic ingredients and an oven-safe skillet or muffin tin.

To make the mini frittatas, start by preheating your oven to 350 degrees Fahrenheit. Then, crack 8 eggs in a large bowl and whisk together with the heavy cream or nut milk, salt, bacon, Parmesan cheese, spinach, and parsley.

Once everything is combined, pour the egg mixture into an oven-safe skillet or muffin tin. Place it in the preheated oven and bake for 15 minutes. When the frittatas are done, let them cool for a few minutes before serving.

Enjoy your healthy mini frittatas as a quick breakfast option or make them ahead of time and store in the fridge for later. They're great on-the-go snacks too! So don't be afraid to give these mini frittatas a try - you won't be disappointed. Bon Appétit!

Breakfast Burritos

Breakfast burritos are a healthy and delicious way to start your kids' day off right. With just a few simple ingredients, you can easily prepare and assemble your own breakfast burrito to fill their tummies and give them the energy they need. Here is how you can make healthy breakfast burritos for your kids in no time.

First, start off by prepping the ingredients: cook the breakfast sausage, scramble the eggs, and chop the bell pepper and green onion. Then warm up the tortillas in a skillet so they're nice and soft.

Next, it's time to assemble the burrito! Place a tortilla on a plate and top with the cooked sausage, eggs, bell pepper, green onion, and cheese. Fold in the sides of the tortilla and then roll it up.

Now your healthy breakfast burrito is ready to serve! These burritos are perfect for kids and adults alike. Enjoy your healthy breakfast burrito with a side of fruit or yogurt, and you'll have a healthy and complete meal. They're also easy to take on-the-go or store in the fridge for later. Enjoy!

Breakfast Skillet

A healthy breakfast skillet is a great option for kids and adults alike. It's an easy-to-prepare, nutritious meal that can be enjoyed any time of day. To make a healthy breakfast skillet, you'll need some frozen hash browns (or grated potatoes), eggs, cheese, and spices.

To start, heat a skillet over medium-high heat and spread the hash browns in an even layer. Cook for about 5 minutes, stirring occasionally to prevent sticking. When the hash browns are golden and crispy, add the eggs (scrambled or fried). Cook until just set and the yolks are still runny.

Next, add the cheese of your choice (cheddar is most common, but feel free to try smoked mozzarella or gouda for a different flavor). Sprinkle some spices like chili powder, garlic, cumin, and fennel seeds. Cook for another few minutes until the cheese melts. Serve warm with some chopped fresh herbs or a side of salsa.

This healthy breakfast skillet is a great way to add some variety to your morning routine and give your kids a nutritious start to the day. Enjoy!

Fried Egg Sandwich

This egg fried sandwich is a healthy and delicious breakfast option for kids. It's easy to prepare and can be enjoyed any day of the week.

Begin by melting the butter in a large skillet over medium-high heat. Once the butter is melted, crack the eggs into the pan and season with salt and pepper to taste. Cook for about 4 minutes or until the eggs are set.

Next, place two slices of cheese on four slices of toasted white bread. Top each slice with one of the cooked eggs and close up the sandwiches.

In a small bowl combine 2 tablespoons mayonnaise and 2 tablespoons ketchup. Spread this mixture onto both sides of each sandwich before returning them to the hot skillet. Cook for 1-2 minutes per side or until golden brown on both sides.

Serve these egg fried sandwiches warm with your favorite condiments and sides. Enjoy!

This healthy breakfast option is a great way to start the day and can be varied to suit everyone's tastes. A few ideas include adding bacon, ham or tomatoes for extra flavor or topping with hot sauce for added spice. Kids will love this delicious breakfast sandwich that's easy to make. Try it today!

Blueberry Smothie

A healthy breakfast is essential for providing energy and nutrients needed to fuel a busy day of activities, especially for growing kids. A blueberry smoothie is an ideal way for children to get the nutrition they need in a tasty, quick way. This recipe calls for just five ingredients and takes only five minutes to prepare.

Start by gathering the necessary ingredients: 1 cup blueberries (frozen or fresh), 1 container plain yogurt, ¾ cup 2% reduced-fat milk, 2 tablespoons white sugar, ½ teaspoon vanilla extract and ⅛ teaspoon ground nutmeg. You can buy all these items at your local grocery store or online.

Blend together all of these ingredients until the mixture is smooth and creamy. If you want to make it extra healthy, substitute the reduced-fat milk with almond or soy milk. You can also use honey instead of white sugar if you prefer a less sweet smoothie.

For an added twist, consider adding other healthy ingredients like kale, spinach, banana or chia seeds - just remember to adjust the liquid levels accordingly. Serve in tall glasses and enjoy! With these simple steps, you can prepare a healthy and delicious breakfast for your kids in no time.

The blueberry smoothie is a healthy and tasty way for children to get their daily dose of vitamins and minerals. With its sweet flavour and creamy texture, this refreshing drink will become your household's go-to morning treat!

Vegetables Scramble

egetable scramble is a healthy and delicious breakfast option for kids. It's easy to prepare and can be customized with different ingredients to make it even more appealing. To make this scrumptious dish, you will need ¼ cup of olive oil, ¼ cup of sliced fresh mushrooms, ¼ cup of chopped onions, ¼ cup of chopped green bell peppers, 6 eggs, ¼ cup of milk, ¼ cup of chopped fresh tomatoes, and ¼ cup of shredded cheddar cheese.

First heat the olive oil in a large skillet over medium-high heat. Add the mushrooms, onions and bell peppers; cook until vegetables are tender. In a medium bowl, whisk together the eggs and milk until blended. Pour the egg mixture into the skillet with the vegetables. Stir continuously to evenly distribute the ingredients and cook until eggs are done. Finally, add in the chopped tomatoes and cheese; stir to combine and melt cheese before serving.

This healthy breakfast will be sure to please even picky eaters. Enjoy!

Bacon And Egg Muffins

Bacon and egg muffins are a healthy breakfast option for kids. Not only are they tasty, but they are also easy to prepare. To make the muffins, you'll need eggs, bacon, cheese, green onions, and any herbs or spices you'd like to add for flavor. Simply whisk all of the ingredients together in a bowl, then portion the mixture into a greased muffin tin. Bake in a preheated oven for about 20 minutes or until lightly golden brown. Serve the muffins warm and with your favorite condiments such as ketchup, hot sauce, or sour cream.

These healthy breakfast muffins can be easily modified to suit different dietary needs, such as omitting the bacon for a vegetarian option. They also make great snack ideas and can be taken on-the-go if you're in a rush. Whether it's starting your day off healthy or packing a healthy snack, these bacon and egg muffins are sure to satisfy everyone!

Chesse Waffles

Cheese waffles are a healthy and delicious breakfast option for kids. Made with simple ingredients, they're also easy to prepare. To make cheese waffles you will need 2 Cups of flour, 2 tsp baking powder, 1 tsp baking soda, 1/2 tsp kosher salt, 2 eggs, 1 1/2 Cup milk, 3 Tbsp vegetable or canola oil, and 1 Cup cheddar cheese, grated.

Firstly, mix the dry ingredients together in a large bowl. In a separate bowl, whisk together the eggs, milk and oil. Then add the wet ingredients to the dry ingredients and stir until combined - it's ok if there are some lumps in the batter. Finally, stir in the grated cheese until it is evenly distributed throughout the batter.

Once the batter is ready, heat up a waffle iron and spray with non-stick cooking spray. Pour about 1/3 cup of batter onto each waffle section and close the lid to cook for 5 minutes or until golden brown. Serve the cheese waffles warm, either with a topping of your choice or as is. Enjoy!

Cheese waffles are an easy and healthy breakfast option for kids that's sure to please the whole family. Try them out today!

Semolina Pudding

Making healthy breakfast options for kids can be a challenge, but this simple and delicious dish of semolina with milk and sugar is an excellent choice. It's easy to prepare and you can make it even more interesting by adding healthy ingredients such as fresh or cooked fruit, dried fruit, chocolate or coconut. To make it, all you need to do is mix the semolina, milk and sugar together in a saucepan on medium heat. Cook until it has thickened up then remove from the heat and allow to cool before serving. For an extra healthy breakfast option, why not try adding some fresh or cooked fruit for flavor and nutrition? You could also sprinkle some dried fruit or coconut over the finished dish for added sweetness and texture. For a truly decadent treat, you could even add some grated chocolate to the top before serving. With so many healthy options available, this semolina breakfast dish will be sure to become a healthy favorite!

Tuna Sandwich

Preparing healthy breakfast for kids doesn't need to be a difficult task. With just a few simple ingredients you can create nutritious, delicious and kid-friendly tuna sandwiches.

To make the sandwich, start by draining two cans of chunk light or albacore white tuna into a bowl. Then add in 1/4 cup of mayonnaise, 1 chopped hard cooked egg, 2 teaspoons of lemon juice, 1/2 cup of chopped celery, 2 tablespoons of sweet pickle relish and 2 teaspoons of lemon pepper seasoning. Mix together until all ingredients are evenly distributed.

Next, take two pieces of bread and spread the tuna mixture onto one slice. Place lettuce leaves on the other slice. Place the slices together and cut. Serve with healthy sides such as sliced tomatoes, carrots or fruit to complete your healthy breakfast for kids. Enjoy!
!

Forest Mushrooms Pate Sandwich

he Forest Mushroom Pâté Sandwich is a healthy and delicious breakfast for kids that is quick to prepare. To make this sandwich, simply butter one side of two slices of bread. Add a thin slice of our Forest Mushroom Pâté, top with a slice of Swiss cheese, a sprinkle of white cheddar cheese, the grilled onions, another slice of Swiss, and finally the other slice of bread. Cook butter-side-down in a nonstick pan until golden brown on each side. Serve with fresh fruit or vegetables for a healthy, balanced meal your kids will love! Enjoy!

Alternatively, you can also prepare this healthy breakfast in a toaster oven by layering all the ingredients between two slices of bread, buttering one side, and baking until golden brown. Whichever way you prefer to make it, your kids will love this healthy breakfast option!

We hope you enjoy making and eating this healthy Forest Mushroom Pâté Sandwich - give it a try today!

Butter And Jam Toast

Toast with butter and jam is a healthy breakfast alternative for kids. Here's how to prepare it:

First, toast two slices of healthy whole-grain bread in the toaster until golden brown. Remove from the toaster and spread liberally with butter so that it melts into the toast. Then, take a knife and spread a thin layer of your favourite healthy jam across the top of the toast. Make sure not to put too much jam on, as it can make for an overly sweet bite. Aim for a 1-2mm screed so that you get the buttery flavour from the toast, with just a hint of fruity sweetness from the jam. Enjoy your healthy breakfast for kids!

Fish Roe Toast

If you're feeling more adventurous, why not try Fish Roe Toast? Start by sifting 50g of flour and 1 teaspoon of cayenne pepper into a bowl. Heat 40g of butter in a pan over medium-high heat and add 450g of soft herring roes. Cook until lightly browned, stirring occasionally. Cut a loaf of crusty bread into slices and spread the cooked roes over the toast. Squeeze fresh lemon juice over the top, and enjoy this healthy breakfast for kids! To make sure that the flavours are well balanced, season with sea salt and black pepper before serving. With these simple ingredients and steps, Fish Roe Toast is easy to make and a healthy breakfast. Bon Appetit!!

Pastrami Sandwich

A healthy and delicious pastrami sandwich is a great way to start the day for kids. To make this flavorful sandwich, you'll need just a few ingredients: rye bloomer or other bread of your choice, mustard, Co-op pastrami beef slices, Swiss cheese or other hard cheese, thin tomato slices, lettuce leaves, mayonnaise, and crisps (optional).

To prepare the sandwich, first spread a teaspoon of mustard on one side of your bread slice. Layer two slices of pastrami beef and two slices of Swiss cheese on top. Arrange some tomato and lettuce leaves over the cheese. Spread mayonnaise on the other side of your bread slice and place it on top of the sandwich. Cut your sandwich into two halves, and serve with crisps or any other side dish of your choice.

This delicious pastrami sandwich can be enjoyed by kids for healthy breakfast or lunch. Preparing this savory sandwich is an easy and fun way to introduce healthy eating habits to your kids. Enjoy!

Bacon Breakfast Pizza

Bacon Breakfast Pizza is a healthy, delicious breakfast that the whole family can enjoy. This pizza combines bacon, mozzarella cheese, garlic, green onions and eggs for a unique taste that your kids will love. Plus, it's ready in just 30 minutes! Here's how to prepare this healthy breakfast pizza:

Start by preheating your oven to 425°F. Spread cornmeal onto a flat surface and roll out the pizza dough until it's about 12-14 inches in diameter. Place the dough on a baking sheet lined with parchment paper and brush with olive oil.

In a skillet over medium heat, cook bacon pieces, stirring occasionally, until crisp and golden brown. Remove from heat, drain on a paper towel-lined plate, then add to the pizza dough along with garlic and green onions. Top with slices of mozzarella cheese, then crack 3 eggs over the top and sprinkle lightly with salt and pepper.

Bake for 15-20 minutes until the edges are golden brown and the eggs are cooked to your liking. Slice, serve and enjoy!

Bacon Breakfast Pizza is a healthy, tasty way to start your day. With just a few simple ingredients, you can make this dish in minutes for a filling breakfast that the whole family will love. Enjoy!

Pumpkin Spice Toast

To prepare the pumpkin spice toast, start by preheating your oven to 350 degrees Fahrenheit and lightly greasing a baking sheet with butter or nonstick cooking spray. Place six slices of brioche bread onto the baking sheet and set aside. In a medium-sized bowl, combine ¼ cup of softened unsalted butter, ¼ cup of pumpkin puree, ¼ cup of granulated sugar, ½ teaspoon of pumpkin pie spice, ¼ teaspoon of cinnamon and a pinch of kosher salt. Use a small spatula to spread the mixture on top of each slice of brioche toast. Place the baking sheet in the preheated oven and bake for 10 minutes, or until the edges of the toast start to turn golden brown.

Remove the baking sheet from the oven and allow the pumpkin spice toast to cool for a few minutes before serving. Enjoy!

This healthy breakfast option is sure to be a hit with kids and adults alike. Serve it with a side of fresh fruit or yogurt for a truly delicious start to the day. Try this pumpkin spice toast and get ready for smiles all around!

Happy cooking! :)
!

Blueberry Sour Cream Pancakes

Blueberry sour cream pancakes are healthy breakfast option for kids that adults can easily prepare. To make these delicious and healthy pancakes, you will need 2 ¼ cups of all-purpose flour, 1 ½ tablespoons sugar, 2 ¼ teaspoons baking powder, ¾ teaspoon baking soda and ¾ teaspoon kosher salt. In a separate bowl, combine 1 cup of whole milk, 1 cup sour cream and 2 large eggs. Whisk these ingredients together until all the lumps have dissolved. Next, mix the dry ingredients into the wet mixture and stir until smooth. Finally, fold in some fresh blueberries before pouring onto a greased griddle or pan over medium heat. Cook until both sides are golden brown and serve with syrup, butter or your favorite toppings. Enjoy!

These blueberry sour cream pancakes provide a healthy breakfast option for kids that is packed full of flavor. With just a few simple ingredients, you can make these delicious pancakes in no time at all. Invite the whole family to the table and treat them to a healthy and hearty breakfast.
Enjoy!

Granola and Yogurt Bowl

A healthy and delicious breakfast for kids is a Granola & Yogurt Bowl. It is easy to prepare and can be tailored to each individual's dietary needs and preferences. To make this healthy meal, start by adding your favorite granola to a bowl. Then, add any of the mentioned richly colored fruits, nuts/seeds, or plain greek yogurt. Finally, top it off with organic milk, soy milk, or almond milk for healthy fats and protein. You can even add a drizzle of honey or maple syrup for an extra touch of sweetness. With all these healthy ingredients, this Granola & Yogurt Bowl is a great way to start the day right! Enjoy as a healthy breakfast for your kids, or as a healthy snack any time of day. Bon Appétit!

Thank you

We hope you enjoyed our book

As a small family company your feedback is very important to us.

Please let us know how you like our book.